KU-726-520

CHOCOLATE
FROSTED FINGERS

CHOCOLATE FROSTED FINGERS

Loving Thoughts from Mom
on Your Birthday

Written by M. K. Moulton
Illustrated by Marsha Winborn

Ideals Publications
Nashville, Tennessee

ISBN 0-8249-5894-2

Published by Ideals Publications
535 Metroplex Drive, Suite 250
Nashville, Tennessee 37211
www.idealsbooks.com

Text copyright © 2006 by Mark Kimball Moulton
Illustrations copyright © 2006 by Marsha Winborn

Color separations by Precision Color Graphics,
Franklin, Wisconsin

Printed and bound in Italy

Designed by Eve DeGrie

10 9 8 7 6 5 4 3 2 1

For my family and friends~
Happy Birthday, one and all! ~M.K.M.

This book is lovingly presented to

Paul

on your birthday.

Love,

Mom

(May you and Ani share the
same joy as Dad & I had....

When you
first came into my life,
I felt my whole world shift.
Somehow I knew
that I'd
been blessed
with life's
most precious gift.

Those next long months were special,
as I waited and I worried.

I longed to hold you in my arms,
but you could not be hurried.

I wondered
what you'd look like;
would you be a boy or girl?

Would you be born with lots of hair
and would it have a curl?

But all

my questions fell away
when I laid eyes
 on you.

I felt a love inside me
that before I never knew.

There you lay,
defenseless,
counting totally on me

for food,
for warmth,
for safety~
I was nervous as can be!

I brought you home.
I did my best.

I made mistakes, I'm sure.

Now, looking back,
I'm not surprised
those first days were a blur.

But soon I got the hang of it~
the burping
and the feeding~

and when I conquered diapering,
I knew I was succeeding.

I noted
your accomplishments
with great parental pride

and showed so many photographs,
my friends all learned to hide!

Your first real smile,
your first haircut,
your first small baby tooth~

I cherish every photo
that I have of your sweet youth.

Some
are touching,
some are sweet,
and some
are just plain fun;

but my very favorite
is of you
the day
that you turned one.

★ ★ ★ ★ ★ ★

We'd just sung "Happy Birthday"
and presented you with cake~

the first you'd ever had alone.
Was that
a big
mistake!

You laughed
and smiled and giggled so~
a child without a care~

with cake and frosting squished between
your hands and in your hair!

And down your front, and on the walls,
and on the chair and floor~

but at that very moment,
I could not have loved you more.

Many years
have come
and gone;
they've slipped by
much too fast.

* * * ⛺ * * *

But every year
you seem
to make me
prouder
than the last.

★ ★ ★ ★ ★ ★

Your first
few steps,
first day at school,
first part in your school play~
every first
still feels just like

it happened yesterday.

Your first
best friend,
your first school dance,
and then your first real date~
each and every memory
is one I celebrate.

You've grown to be
a person I admire and respect,

one who'll make a difference
in this big world, I suspect.

✦ ✦ ✦ 🎉 ✦ ✦ ✦

My love for you
will never change,
no matter what
 your age.

★ ★ ★ ★ ★ ★

You'll always be my own
bright little star on center stage.

So on this
very special,
most auspicious,
grand occasion,

I'm filled with joy
to make a wish
for you in celebration.

I wish you
all the happiness
that I have found in you,

and hope
that every happy dream
will be a dream come true.

I wish you
health and peace of mind,
the pleasure of good friends,

contentment and security,
and love
that never ends.

In short, I wish you
all the joy you felt
when you turned one.

Go revel in the gift of life~
you've only just begun!

But if I may,
there's some advice
that I would like to share:

try to keep the frosting
and the cake out of your hair!